TECHNOLOGY

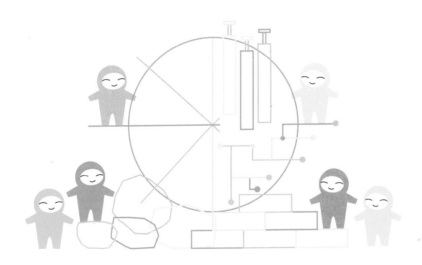

KINGFISHER

NEW YORK

KINGFISHER
LONDON & NEW YORK

Copyright © Kingfisher 2012
Published in the United States by Kingfisher,
175 Fifth Ave., New York, NY 10010
Kingfisher is an imprint of Macmillan Children's Books, London.

Distributed in the U.S. and Canada by Macmillan, 175 Fifth Ave., New York, NY 10010

Consultant: Professor Barrett Hazeltine, Professor Emeritus, Brown University

Designed and created by Basher www.basherbooks.com
Text written by Dan Green

Dedicated to Stan, Samuel, Joel, Jude, Martha, and Naomi

Library of Congress Cataloging-in-Publication data has been applied for.

ISBN: 978-0-7534-6820-3

Kingfisher books are available for special promotions and premiums.
For details contact: Special Markets Department, Macmillan, 175 Fifth Ave., New York, NY 10010.

For more information, please visit www.kingfisherbooks.com

Printed in China
9 8 7 6 5 4 3 2
2TR/0512/WKT/UNTD/140MA

Contents

Introduction
Technology

Glittering, gleaming, and winking at you from all angles, technology is everywhere. Just take a look—almost every human-made thing you see is an invention! Usually designed to solve a problem or make a task easier, technology can also help you have fun. Always looking to the future, it uses science to make more useful materials and better, more efficient machines.

 The great-granddaddy of all inventors was the ancient Greek brainiac Archimedes (c. 287–212 B.C.), the original gadget geek. (No doubt he'd be bitterly disappointed to read this because he always fancied himself as a great mathematician.) But he just couldn't stop inventing great gizmos. The Archimedean screw is still used today to lift water and is the guiding principle behind a ship's propeller. His "death ray" used mirrors to concentrate the Sun's energy onto Roman ships while a giant claw tipped them over backward! Once upon a time, the cutting edge of high tech was a chariot or a boat made of grass. But who knows what's coming next—hover shoes, self-cleaning clothes, remote-controlled rain?

Archimedes

CHAPTER 1
Movers 'n' Shakers

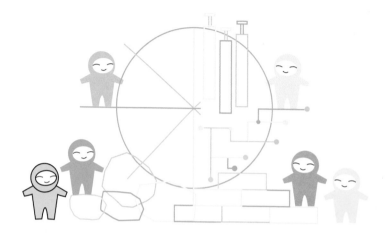

Some of these mini marvels have been around a very long time—and with good reason. Each one is a regular superhero, saving you work by swinging mechanical advantage your way. These guys allow you to move a heavy load over a short distance with little effort. So what's their secret? It lies in transforming a low-force, long-distance input into a high-force, short-distance output. That's how little ole Screw and Lever manage to lift a car in a jackscrew. It's time to find out how these pint-size heroes operate. No mechanical contraption could work without them! Ready to let them loose?

Wheel
and Axle

Gears

Screw

Rack and
Pinion

Bearing

Lever

Pulley

Hydraulics

Spring

Control System

Wheel and Axle

■ Movers 'n' Shakers

☀ Circular wheel is connected to machinery by rodlike axle
☀ Together they make possible the forward motion of vehicles
☀ Rolling is easier than sliding, so the force required to move is less

Hey there, let's start this thing rollin'! We are the winning combo that really gets people on the move. Rickshaws and racers, scooters and skateboards—anything that uses a disk shape to trundle along sets our unique skills in motion. We're a "wheely" good invention!

Just imagine how important simple rollers are for factory conveyor belts, moving sidewalks, and baggage carousels. Sure, Wheel does all the work, but it would be useless without sturdy Axle connecting that dizzy disk to the mechanism. Most axles sit dead center, allowing Wheel to spin freely. Placed off center, though, Axle makes a special device called a cam, which has an up-and-down element to its movement. Think wobbly pull toy and you've got it. Rock 'n' roll!

● First wheel-and-axle combination: c.3500 B.C. (chariot)
● Wheel-and-axle applications: water wheel, doorknob, rotary whisk, fishing reel
● World's first Ferris wheel: 1893 (Chicago World's Fair)

Wheel and Axle

Gears

☀ Transmit motion from one part of a machine to another
☀ When engaged, turning one gear causes the next to rotate
☀ Change speed and create mechanical advantage

All "geared" up, we are characters with real drive. We transfer energy from power source to wheel. We run like clockwork and once we're on a roll, there's no stopping us!

You may be familiar with the cog—a wheel with straight teeth around its outer edge—but there are also bevel gears (where slanting teeth transfer motion around a corner) and worm gears (shafts with a screw thread). We're "engaging" fellows and love to mesh with others of our kind. A small gear driving a larger one needs to rotate many times to get the larger one to turn once. This slows the motion but also requires less force to drive. (Car transmissions work like this.) Mechanical timepieces use us in exacting combos to drive both of their hands accurately at different speeds. We've got the gear!

● Transmission: two or more gears operating together
● Gear ratio: relationship between the number of times that meshed gears rotate
● World's longest two-wheeled bicycle: 92.2 ft (28.1m)

Gears

Screw
■ Movers 'n' Shakers

- ☀ An axle with a sloped spiral track called a thread
- ☀ The thread converts rotary motion to linear motion
- ☀ Works with a gear to turn direction of rotation through 90°

I'm totally screwy! Whirling and twirling, I'm a clever little device made from a sloping surface that winds around a cylinder. Wrap a right-angled triangle made from paper around a pencil and you'll see exactly how I turn.

As I rotate, my sloped thread transfers circular motion to horizontal motion. In doing so, it reduces the distance traveled for the same effort, bringing more forceful drive. With every glorious twist, I move forward, and this allows my thread to bite and worm its way easily into wood. I'm best known for the short, sharp metal spikes that fix one thing to another, but look around and you'll find me in screw-top lids, in propeller blades, cooling fans, and corkscrews. Once you start looking, you'll find my spiraling forms utterly mesmerizing!

- ● World's first screw: 200s B.C. (Archimedean screw, ancient Greece)
- ● First screw-cutting lathe: 1770 (Jess Ramsden, U.K.)
- ● Invention of the Phillips screw: 1930s (Henry Phillips, U.S.)

Screw

Rack and Pinion

■ Movers 'n' Shakers

* A partnership of a gear and a flat, toothed plate
* Converts horizontal movement to rotary motion, or vice versa
* Pulls funicular trains up steep slopes where wheels would slide

What an awesome duo! With us in control, you'll always be heading in the right direction. Circular, toothed Pinion meshes with playmate Rack (like Gear, but with the teeth unwound and laid flat). When Pinion rotates, Rack moves to one side or the other. Together we form the steering system in motor vehicles, allowing the wheel to move the wheels (if you follow).

Rack and Pinion

● First rack-and-pinion (cog) railway: 1812 (Middleton Railway, Leeds, U.K.)
● Steepest funicular railway: 48% (Pilatus Railway, Switzerland)
● First patent on rack-and-pinion steering: 1975 (Arthur E. Bishop, Australia)

Bearing

Movers 'n' Shakers

☀ Reduces friction in the workings of a machine
☀ Fitted to axles, it allows wheels and gears to move freely
☀ Some of these fluid movers need a little lubrication

Bearing

A *smooooth* operator, I make machinery run effortlessly and noiselessly. I may be a strip of metal or plastic sandwiched between two contact surfaces. Or, perhaps, the more fancy ball or caged roller bearings (which work because things roll better than they slide). You'll find me nestling in your bike wheel hubs or killing time (and friction) in your watch to keep it spot-on!

● First caged roller bearings: 1740s (John Harrison, U.K.)
● First patent on ball bearings: 1869 (Jules Suriray, France)
● Jewel bearings: used by watchmakers to reduce energy lost to friction

Lever
■ Movers 'n' Shakers

* ☀ A simple device for changing the size of a force
* ☀ Made up of a rigid length and a pivot
* ☀ Generally grouped in three different classes

Straight as a rod, I'm a pushy so-and-so. I can amplify your effort to give you superstrength or reduce it so that you don't crush itty-bitty things. All you need to get some leverage is a rod and a pivot (called a fulcrum).

With my three classes of levers, I can move the earth! Class one levers, such as a crowbar, place the fulcrum in between your applied force and the thing you want to move. Even the puniest effort will prize the lid off a can or jimmy open a heavy door in no time. A wheelbarrow is a class two lever, with the fulcrum at one end, your force at the other, and the load in between. It makes lifting heavy goods a breeze. A baseball bat is a class three lever. With the fulcrum at one end and the load at the other, it magnifies your effort to send a ball flying. Wowzer!

* ● Scissors: a pair of class one levers pivoted around the same fulcrum
* ● Nutcrackers: a pair of class two levers joined at the fulcrum
* ● Tweezers: a pair of class three levers joined at the fulcrum

Lever

Pulley

■ Movers 'n' Shakers

❋ A clever rope-over-grooved-wheel combo
❋ Makes light work of hoisting and carrying heavy loads
❋ Two or more pulleys put together are called block and tackle

Check out my muscle! My smart system of passing a line over a grooved wheel changes the direction of your effort. Pull *down* on my rope and a bucket of water rises *up* out of a well. I'm used for raising flags or closing curtains, and, famously, in cranes. With the cable doubled and running over several pulleys, a crane is able to lift stupendous weights. "Groove-y" man!

Pulley

● Fixed pulley: changes only the direction of force
● Movable pulley: free to move in space and so gives mechanical advantage
● World's strongest crane: 22,000-ton (20,000-metric-tonne) capacity (Taisun)

Hydraulics

Movers 'n' Shakers

* This athlete operates on high-pressure fluid power
* Employed to transmit force precisely
* Used for vehicle brake and power-steering systems

Hydraulics

Welcome to the rollickin', *hydraulickin'* world of sealed cylinders, each one a fluid-filled barrel with a piston inside. Press the brake pedal of a car and you put the fluid on one side of the piston under pressure. The piston moves away to equalize the pressure while a rod connected to the piston transmits the movement as a forceful push to ja-ja-jam on the brakes.

● Invention of the hydraulic press: 1795 (Joseph Bramah, U.K.)
● Common applications: bus doors, dump trucks, and arms of excavators
● Largest excavator: 1,836-cu.-ft. (52m³) bucket capacity (Bucyrus RH400)

Spring
■ Movers 'n' Shakers

※ This bouncy fellow stores mechanical energy when deformed
※ Perfect for uncoupling vibrations between two objects
※ Flat and coiled springs are usually made of hardened steel

Howdy! You know me—the dude that makes jumping up and down on the bed soooo much fun! Anything elastic gets to be in my gang—just as long as it gives bounce-back! Say hello to the longbow, wooden springboard, and pliers, all just as much springs as my more usual squashy, stretchy, flexible coils of metal.

I come in three main types: compression (squashed short); extension (stretched long); and torsion (tightened in a spiral). It takes energy to squash, stretch, or twist me, but do I bend out of shape? No way! I store the effort in my loops and deliver it right back when I spring. I provide the power to keep spring-driven watches going and help machines such as click-top pens and brushes in motors maintain tension between parts. Boy, I need to unwind!

● Applications: jack-in-the-box (compression); Slinky (extension); mousetrap (torsion)
● Invention of the innerspring mattress: 1871 (Heinrich Westphal, Germany)
● Hooke's law: the force that a spring exerts is proportional to its change in length

Spring

Control System
Movers 'n' Shakers

✴ Uses system-controlling devices to regulate a machine
✴ Mechanical or electronic action is triggered by feedback
✴ Often used in safety mechanisms or fail-safe devices

I'm the governor. I crack the whip that gets the Movers 'n' Shakers running like clockwork. They do a good job, but they're not smart—you can't switch off a bouncing fool like Spring! No, most machines combine two or more parts, and I monitor and control how they operate.

My genius lies in having two parts—sensor and actuator. The sensor provides information about the output of a machine by measuring properties such as light, temperature, or pressure. The actuator device alters the operation and may do so by mechanical means (say a rack and pinion or a hydraulic valve) or through an electrical circuit. So when Refrigerator's thermostat senses that the temperature is rising too high, the actuator operates an electrical switch to turn on the compressor. My simple click does the trick!

● First feedback control device: 300 B.C. (water clock of Ktesibios, Egypt)
● Bang-bang controller: switches abruptly from one state (on) to another (off)
● Examples of a bang-bang control system: refrigerator, residential heating

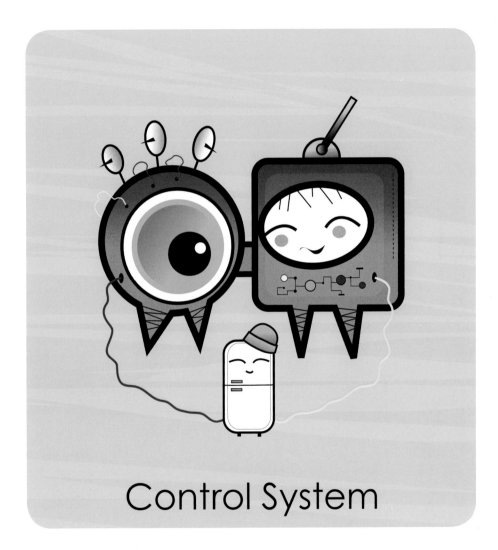

Control System

CHAPTER 2
Homebodies

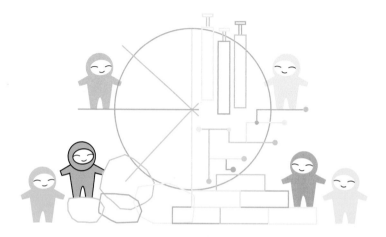

You rub shoulders with these housemates every day. They are so much a part of your life that you probably cannot imagine the world without them. With CD and DVD around, you probably don't have much time for fusty old Radio, but don't be fooled. This old-timer has hidden talents, making Television's job possible and doing most of the legwork for hotshot Microwave Oven. Beat that for a technology supposedly on its last legs! Light Bulb lights up your life, and Telephone chitchats away. Refrigerator helps you eat well, while toiler Toilet . . . well, the less said the better! Face it, Homebodies rule—let's find out more.

Radio

Television

Light Bulb

Refrigerator

Microwave Oven

Telephone

Toilet

Clock

CD and DVD

Radio
◼ Homebodies

✴ This dude excels as a global wireless communicator
✴ Streams electromagnetic waves through the air
✴ Uses a transmitter and receiver to get the message across

When it comes to being connected, there's no one like me, baby! Invisible radio waves zap music, news, moving pictures, and chat speedily and silently across the globe. You know me best as the receiver of these airwaves—a radio set—but I transmit as well as receive great vibes.

Vibrating radio waves are generated by an electronic circuit (transmitter) and whiz through space, bouncing back and forth between satellites. All you need is an antenna: my waves get electrons buzzing in the metal antenna, and this electric current is converted into sound or vision (receiver). A simple telegraph uses Morse code's blips and beeps, but I can be modulated—by a second radio wave, called a carrier (AM/FM on your radio), or digitally—to deliver voice and music. Ah, sweet sounds!

● First working radio: 1894 (Oliver Lodge, U.K.)
● First transatlantic radio signal: 1901 (Guglielmo Marconi, Italy)
● Speed of radio waves: 983,571,056 ft./sec. (299,792,458m/s)

Radio

Television
■ Homebodies

✳ A splendiferous moving-picture entertainer
✳ Uses radio waves to pipe TV shows into your home
✳ This global channel-surfer is changing to digital transmission

The house entertainer, I'm just bursting with hyperactive, multicolored, thousand-watt brightness! I'll tell you what the weather's up to, I'll keep you right up to date with events and I'll even do a little educatin' while I'm at it!

I use Radio's electromagnetic waves to carry my fab broadcasts. They're transmitted in channels using ultra-high frequencies (UHF). Each channel has two signals—one for pictures and one for sound. When picked up by a receiver (your TV), Radio's waves convert into electrical signals. These activate a color grid to make pictures on your screen. Today's plasma, LCD, and LED screens use hundreds of thousands of tiny lamps to do this. The picture updates 50 to 60 times a second to give the appearance of movement. Lights, camera . . . action!

● First demonstration of moving pictures: 1925 (John Logie Baird, U.K.)
● Number of world's households with at least one TV: 1.2 billion
● TV frequency band: 470–854 MHz

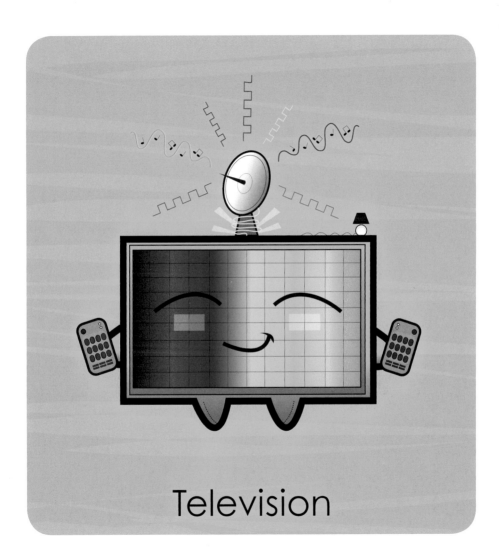

Television

Light Bulb
■ Homebodies

☀ One of the world's most important innovations
☀ This bright spark radically changed the lives of our ancestors
☀ Incandescent light bulbs waste electrical energy as heat

I am totally switched on—inventing me was such a bright idea! Of all the Homebodies, I've had the single greatest impact on people's lives. Before me, lighting up after dark was messy—much better to hit the sack at nightfall.

With me in your house, you can stay up late. I make the streets safer after dark and double the working day for manufacturers! An early version of me is the incandescent bulb. A thin metal wire sits within my glass body and glows white hot when an electric current passes through it. I'm filled with an unreactive gas, such as argon, to stop it from catching fire. But that's not so *bright* after all! I convert only 10 percent of the energy into light. My newer, fluorescent bulbs use five times less energy and last about ten times longer. Light fantastic!

● First light bulb patent: 1841 (Frederick de Moleyns, U.K.)
● Energy conversion of an incandescent bulb: 90% (heat); 10% (light)
● Energy conversion of a compact fluorescent light bulb: 30% (heat); 70% (light)

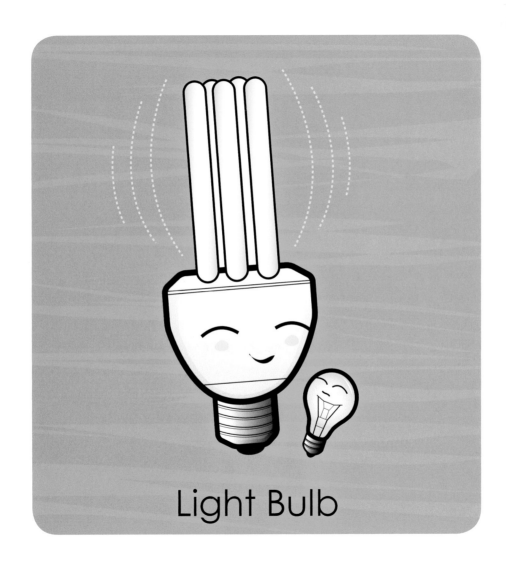

Light Bulb

Refrigerator
■ Homebodies

☀ This cool operator uses a simple heat pump for its inner chill
☀ Keeps drinks and food fresh and slows bacterial attack
☀ A freezer works on the same principle but at a colder setting

The k-k-king of cool, you'll find me chillin' in the kitchen, stuffed full of yummy munchies. A real hit with the whole family, I keep food fresh for much longer, allowing you all to have a delicious balanced diet.

Do you hear my motor running? That's my compressor hard at work moving heat from my insides to the outside. It works by compressing a special gas until it becomes a liquid. This liquid is then pumped inside me, where it turns back into gas, taking heat with it, just like evaporating sweat cools your forehead. Back outside, the gas is compressed again and a metal grid radiator helps me lose the heat to the air (which is why I am always hot around the back). When the fluid returns to room temperature, it is compressed and the cycle begins again. No sweat!

● Invention of the first practical fridge: 1876 (Carl von Linde, Germany)
● Optimum fridge temperature: 37 °F–41 °F (3 °C–5 °C)
● Before the invention of the fridge, cold salt water was used as a refrigerant

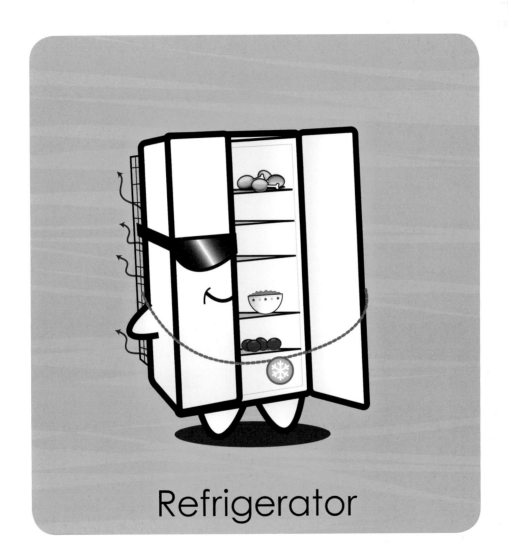

Refrigerator

Microwave Oven

■ Homebodies

☀ This speedy whiz knows all there is to know about *fast* food
☀ Uses energetic radio waves to heat up your meals
☀ The food is heated internally so it does not brown

Hungry and in a hurry? Well, look no further! I cook with lightning speed, taking food from frozen to fiery in a flash. I'm the king of reheat and the prince of popcorn!

I use a device called a magnetron to generate high-frequency radio waves. They are channeled into my oven and scattered by a rotating fan. These microwaves are absorbed by water, fat, and sugar molecules in food, making them rotate in the changing electric field. The more the molecules vibrate, the hotter the food becomes. My design means I can't help setting up hot spots of concentrated radio waves, so I have a rotating carousel to make sure I cook evenly. Put a plate of marshmallows on a nonspinning piece of cardboard and you'll see these hot spots magically appear. Spooky!

● Invention of the magnetron: 1943 (John Randall, U.K.)
● First commercial microwave oven: 1954
● Microwave frequency: 2.45 GHz

Microwave Oven

Telephone
■ Homebodies

✹ Telecom device that transmits encoded sound as electricity
✹ Lets you tell someone you love them when they are far away
✹ Hooks up the planet's countries to help them do business

Yackety-yak! I'm a chatty guy who likes to bring people together. I've made the world smaller by letting folks talk to one another when they are apart.

When you pick up my handset, a local exchange powers it up, connects a digit-receiving device to the line, and produces a dial tone to tell you that I'm ready. The exchange decodes the number you punch in and sends a pulsed signal if the line is free (riiiing). Picking my partner up at the other end completes the circuit, and you can shoot the breeze for as long as you like! My circuitry converts your gabfest into electrical signals that are carried on copper wires from your home. Fiber-optic Cable helps carry data from local exchanges, while Radio sends international calls via Satellite. Zappety-zap!

● First patented telephone: 1876 (Alexander Graham Bell, U.S.)
● First coast-to-coast telephone call in the U.S.: 1915
● First pay phone created: 1889 (William Gray, U.S.)

Telephone

Toilet
■ Homebodies

✳ Teams up with sewers to make our lives cleaner
✳ Public toilets feature infrared-controlled automatic flushing
✳ Dry toilets and dual-flush toilets are green innovations

I'm an unassuming guy and yet I am put upon and sat on all the time. I'm the stalwart that carries your mess away, keeping the bathroom, street, and neighborhood smelling sweet. It's a dirty job, but someone has to do it. I do it very well, as it happens, and I'm *flushed* with pride!

Everyone needs to go at some point, and I'm there when you need me. I come in many types, from sit-down throne to the squat toilet, to the tiny aircraft lavatory and the space-age, self-cleaning booth. Most flushing toilets use a system popularized by Victorian plumber Mr. Thomas Crapper. The handle opens a valve, releasing water from the tank into the bowl. A float controls the water level in the tank, triggering a fill valve to open when the float falls and to close when the tank is full.

● First flushing system: 1596 (John Harington, U.K.)
● Average tank capacity of a modern toilet: 1.5 gal (6L)
● Estimated world population without access to a proper toilet: 2.6 billion

Toilet

Clock
■ Homebodies

☀ This steady character always makes a timely appearance
☀ Operates using a mechanism called an oscillator
☀ The more accurate the oscillator, the more precise the clock

Tick. Tock. Can't. Stop. A stickler for punctuality, I keep the world ticking over. I like everything to run on time. Oh yes, without me there'd be chaos, I tell you. Chaos!

My many forms work using the same basic components. The key is my oscillator—a mechanism that produces regularly spaced pulses. In mechanical timepieces, this may be a pendulum, while electronic clocks have a vibrating quartz crystal. The oscillator is kept going by a power source, such as gravity, batteries, or household electricity. Oscillators produce many pulses per second, sometimes more than 32,000, so a mechanism for counting one pulse a second is needed. Gears do this in a mechanical watch. And then comes the best part: an indicator (my beautiful face) tells you what the time is!

● First mechanical clock: 1088 (Song Dynasty water clock, China)
● First digital clock: 1968 (Peter Petrov, U.S.)
● Most reliable: NIST quantum logic clock (accurate to 1 sec. in 3.7 billion years)

Clock

CD and DVD
■ Homebodies

☀ These party starters are big on the digital data storage scene
☀ Consist of a layer of aluminum sandwiched between plastic
☀ Each of them is read optically using a laser

Introducing . . . the sound and vision duo! Man, we bring the party! A rockin' mode of data storage, you'll find us packing music, movies, games, and so much more.

CD started the revolution by converting sound waves into digital code—gone are those scratchy analog formats, tape and vinyl. And what CD did for sound, DVD did for vision. Both work the same way: a layer of polycarbonate plastic is etched with pits in a spiral from the center to the outer edge. The pattern of pits contains the data. On top of this goes a shiny layer of aluminum and a protective lacquer. When a laser is shone up through the polycarbonate and bounced off the aluminum, an electrical signal is generated by the changes in reflectivity caused by the pits. Starting to get the picture?

● CD: compact disc; DVD: digital versatile disc
● First music album released on CD: 1982 (*52nd Street*, Billy Joel)
● First movie released on DVD: 1997 (*Twister*)

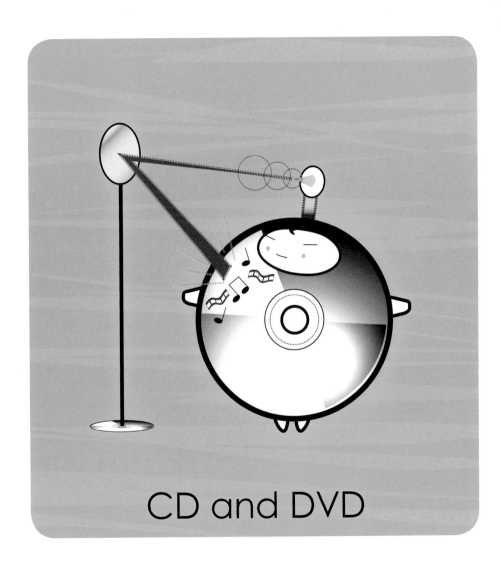

CD and DVD

CHAPTER 3
Mega Materials

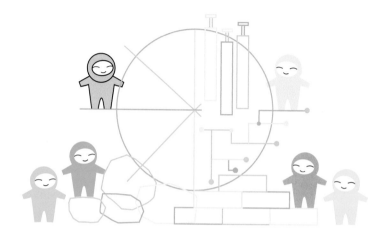

Wow! These guys are ace-in-the-hole magicians with a host of tricks up their sleeves. The Mega Materials are the stuff that many things are made of, and their properties are what make them so important. Strength, hardness, being waterproof or flexible—each of these guys has one or more amazing characteristic that makes it suitable for particular uses. There's no point in making a car out of wobbly silica gel! The magic lies in taking raw materials—the stuff we find in and on Earth—in their natural states and turning them into useful substances. Well, these fellows are just right for the job. C'mon! Let's find out what they do.

Paper

Concrete

Steel

Plastic

Ceramics

Fertilizer

Explosives

Smart Materials

Paper
■ Mega Materials

※ A thin sheet used for writing on, wrapping up, or even as food
※ Made in a paper mill out of a mesh of tiny cellulose fibers
※ Comes mostly from softwood trees such as spruce and pine

I am a starchy original. For centuries, people have come to me in search of knowledge. Books, newspapers, and letters may be the greatest of my incarnations, but I also make paper money, kleenex, and tracing paper.

I'm one of the great inventions of ancient China. "Wood" you believe I get made from mashed-up trees? Under a microscope, you can see my interlocking cellulose fibers. This stuff builds the woody parts of trees and helps them stay upright. I'm made by pulping the wood before cooking it with acid to break down the cells. I'm dyed and put onto rollers, then heated, vacuum-dried, and compressed to the right thickness before emerging as a big roll, ready for cutting. Textiles are used to make paper money in a similar way—from rags to riches, you might say!

● Most common use: packaging (41% of all paper used)
● Number of newspapers from an average tree: about 800
● Amount of paper recycled per year in the U.S.: 45 million tons (2010)

Paper

Concrete
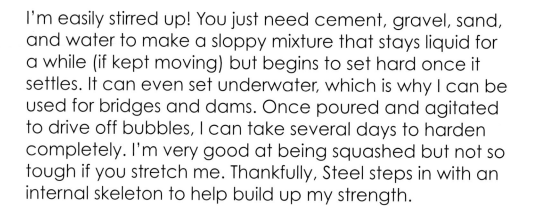
■ Mega Materials

✳ Hard-nut composite material invented by the Romans
✳ This cement-aggregate mix solidifies when added to water
✳ Hardens over years by reacting with carbon dioxide in the air

I'm a mixing marvel. I may not be beautiful (especially in the rain), but I am certainly cheap, and that has made me the planet's most popular building material. Together with Steel, I have built the modern world—bridges, roads, skyscrapers, dams, pipes, and even ships. All me, me, me!

I'm easily stirred up! You just need cement, gravel, sand, and water to make a sloppy mixture that stays liquid for a while (if kept moving) but begins to set hard once it settles. It can even set underwater, which is why I can be used for bridges and dams. Once poured and agitated to drive off bubbles, I can take several days to harden completely. I'm very good at being squashed but not so tough if you stretch me. Thankfully, Steel steps in with an internal skeleton to help build up my strength.

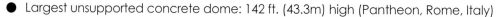

● Largest unsupported concrete dome: 142 ft. (43.3m) high (Pantheon, Rome, Italy)
● Invention of modern concrete: 1756 (John Smeaton, U.K.)
● Invention of reinforced concrete: 1849 (Joseph Monier, France)

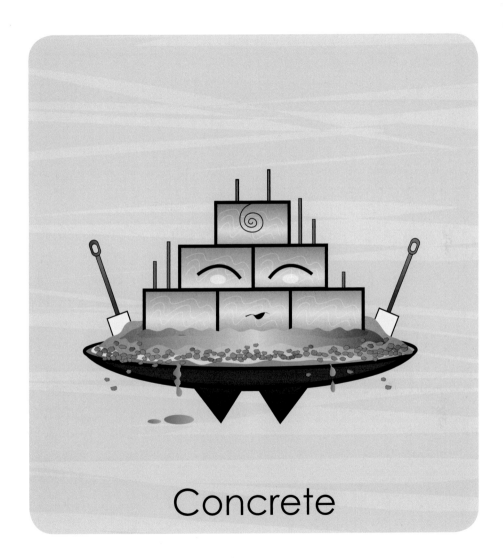

Concrete

Steel
■ Mega Materials

* ☀ Hard-as-nails alloy made from iron mixed with a little carbon
* ☀ Popular because iron is so cheap to mine and extract
* ☀ Combines with hardy concrete to build skyscrapers

A mighty, heighty tower of strength, I build the world's tallest buildings. A thousand times stronger than pure iron, I'm used for everything from knives, tools, and flatware to trains, office buildings, and transmission towers.

I am made in a Bessemer furnace, where molten iron is blasted with oxygen to remove impurities such as sulfur and phosphorus. Modern furnaces convert a staggering 350 tons (318 tonnes) of iron into steel in less than half an hour. Imagine that! A low carbon content makes me tough but easily shaped, while a higher carbon content makes me harder and more brittle. I am further enhanced with the addition of other elements. Chromium prevents me from rusting, while manganese makes me tough enough for use in rails and rock crushers. I am the Man of Steel!

* ● Typical carbon content (by weight): 1.2%–2%
* ● Amount of steel made per year: 1.3 billion tons (1.2 billion metric tonnes)
* ● World's tallest steel-framed building: 2,717 ft. (828m) (Burj Khalifa, Dubai, U.A.E.)

Steel

Plastic
■ Mega Materials

☀ Modern material made from plants or refined crude oil
☀ Classed as thermosoftening plastics and thermosetting plastics
☀ Cheap, moldable, and very durable, with multiple uses

I am one bright and cheery dude, with an amazing ability to mold to any shape. My many forms are made from polymers—atoms joined together in long, flexible chains. Most are hydrocarbon chains with additives that determine color, hardness, flexibility, or weight. Get me!

Thermosetting plastics are molded when hot and stay in shape when they cool, even if heated again. With thermosoftening plastics, however, the polymers can slide over each other and be remolded every time they are heated. I really get around. I make the casings for electrical gizmos and home appliances and am used in the construction business. You'll find me in cars, planes, boats, fabrics, toys, and packaging. But I tend to hang around and have gotten a bad rep for pollution. Pity!

● First man-made plastic: 1856 (Parkesine, Alexander Parkes, U.K.)
● Amount of plastic trash in the oceans: 46,000 pieces per sq. mi. (2.59km^2)
● Average lifespan of a plastic bottle: 300–500 years

Plastic

Ceramics
Mega Materials

* A hard and brittle gang made of nonmetallic crystals
* Molded into shape and then fired hard with heat
* Range from old-school pottery to high-tech materials

Ancient in origin, we have stood the test of time. We are smooth, glassy, and cold—hard enough to stop a bullet, resistant to chemical attack, and impervious to heat.

Sounds impressive? Well, there's more! Unlike many materials, we refuse to be bent and built on and are simply too hard to be cut or shaped. While tough when compressed, we're brittle and shatter easily. Because of this, we each tend to be cast as a single piece—a perfect individual. The first ceramic materials were clay, which contains kaolinite minerals. Today's advanced ceramics use crystals of silicon carbide, zinc oxide, zirconia, and silicon nitride. These make fantastically durable parts that have many uses, from car disc brakes to bulletproof vests. Gotta like the shape of that!

● Temperature range for firing ceramics: 1,800 °F–3,000 °F (1,000 °C–1,600 °C)
● Common ancient uses: pots, tiles, tableware, decorative figures
● Modern-day uses: blades, turbine rotors, insulators, bearings, semiconductors

Ceramics

Fertilizer
■ Mega Materials

* ❋ This farming favorite makes barren land fertile
* ❋ Allows the ground to be used year after year without a break
* ❋ Promotes copious growth of roots, leaves, shoots, and flowers

Oooh! I love to feel the soil between my toes. Spread over fields, I put back into the dirt the elements that growing plants take out. Without me, the land wouldn't support decent crops for long. But don't mess with me. Used too much, I make soil too acidic to grow plants and cause algal blooms in waterways that use up all the oxygen and stifle life. You have been warned!

Fertilizer

* ● First factory-made fertilizer: 1842 (superphosphate, U.K.)
* ● Organic fertilizers: horse manure, guano (seabird dung), powdered limestone
* ● Inorganic fertilizers: ammonia, phosphate pentoxide (from rock phosphorus)

Explosives

Mega Materials ■

* Materials that cause rapid and violent chemical reactions
* Release energy as pressure, sound, heat, and light
* Useful for blasting rocks to reveal Earth's riches

Explosives

Living life on the edge, we have a nasty habit of going off with a BANG! Our destructive power comes from the energy stored in our chemical bonds. Many of us are based on elements that join together very tightly—nitrogen, carbon, and oxygen. When their bonds break, they release their energy very quickly in a rush of expanding gases and heat. It's a blast!

● Invention of gunpowder: 800s B.C. (China)
● Detonation speeds of commercial explosives: 5,900–26,250 ft./sec. (1,800–8,000m/s)
● Largest (nonnuclear) explosion: 6 kilotons of TNT (N1 rocket launch, 1969, U.S.S.R.)

Smart Materials
Mega Materials

* Visionary types that respond to changing conditions
* Some claim to have self-healing properties
* Further development of these smarties will change the world

A bunch of new materials containing whizzo particles, we are real smart cookies. Compared with our meager Mega Materials pals, we're far out. We're the future, my friend!

We are able to change in appearance, behavior, or shape according to conditions around us—temperature, stress, electric and magnetic fields, or acidity, say. Many of our applications are futuristic, but you may know some of us already. One of our gang includes voltage-sensitive (electrochromic) material in LCDs that changes the color and transparency of Television's screen. Sharp, eh? Then there are shape-memory alloys that *remember* the form of your eyeglasses, even if you squash 'em. Some day, toilet seats will warm up when you sit on them and your car will be able to change color to suit your mood!

● Photomechanical materials respond to a change in light conditions
● Piezoelectric materials change size with electricity
● Halochromic materials respond to a change in acidity

Smart Materials

CHAPTER 4
Groovy Gizmos

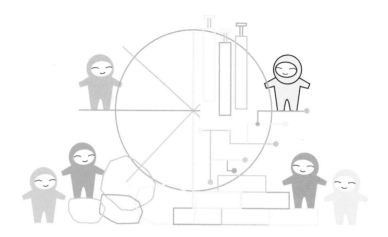

This crew includes tiny prizefighters who punch well above their weight. Because they have fitted so comfortably into everyday life, it's easy to overlook just how much of a shakeup these Groovy Gizmos have caused. These heroes sparked the digital revolution—a method of encoding and manipulating information that has led to an incredible explosion of technology. Digital devices deal with information as strings of ones and zeros that are really electrical pulses—"on" (1) and "off" (0). None does this better than mighty Microchip, a stringpuller extraordinaire. It's time to find out why.

Microchip

Mobile Phone

Computer

User Interface

Digital Camera

Flash Memory

Microchip
Groovy Gizmos

☀ Semiconducting electronic circuit found in all electronic gizmos
☀ A billion transistors can fit on a thumbnail-size microchip
☀ This mini genius is also known as an integrated circuit

Get *me*! I am the master of all gadgetry, the crux at the core of all electronic devices. My mini circuits are shrunk onto tiny slabs of silicon and built up into eye-wateringly complex combinations of components.

I'm a tiny fellow but, boy, do I pack a punch. I call the shots inside your laptop, cell phone, MP3 player, and game console. Without me, those Gizmos have no groove! I reduce every request to a sequence of simple calculations and logic operations. The secret of my genius lies in the transistor—basically, a switch that is controlled by the state of other switches. When current passes through a transistor, we say its state is 1; otherwise the state is 0. These 1s and 0s are bits. The binary code of bits is the basis of all operations. Pretty special, right?

● Typical transistor density: 1 million transistors per square mm
● A byte: a sequence of eight bits
● A nibble: half a byte

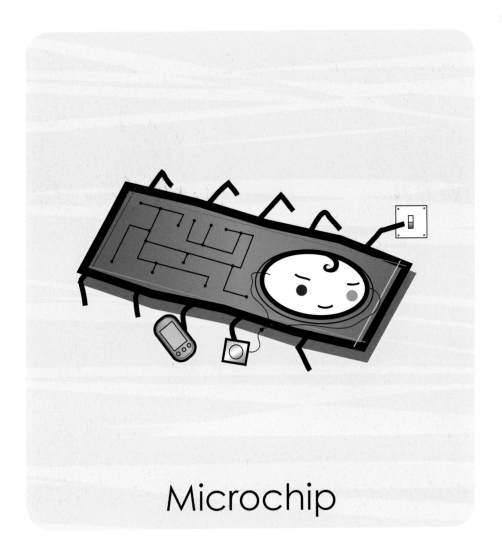

Microchip

Cell Phone
Groovy Gizmos

※ Roaming communications device using a network of cells
※ Sometimes holds personal and security details on a SIM card
※ Has changed society and revolutionized life in far-off places

I'm a free-range bird—I simply love to roam. Thanks to me you can keep in touch with your friends when you're on the go. It's a very *moving* thought!

I provide a service that allows you to make calls or send texts, and I use Radio's waves to zap them through space. Highly charged Battery powers me up and User Interface helps push the right buttons. Coverage comes via a network of "cells," each with a tower in the center. When you make a call, I find the tower with the strongest signal and communicate with it. Each cell operates on its own frequency, and my clever circuitry handles the complex business of switching frequencies as you move between cells. I do it seamlessly, without losing the signal. Not a word is lost, so you never notice it happening!

● SIM: subscriber identity module
● World's first call made from a cell phone: 1973 (U.S.)
● First phone-to-phone SMS (short message service) text message: 1993 (Finland)

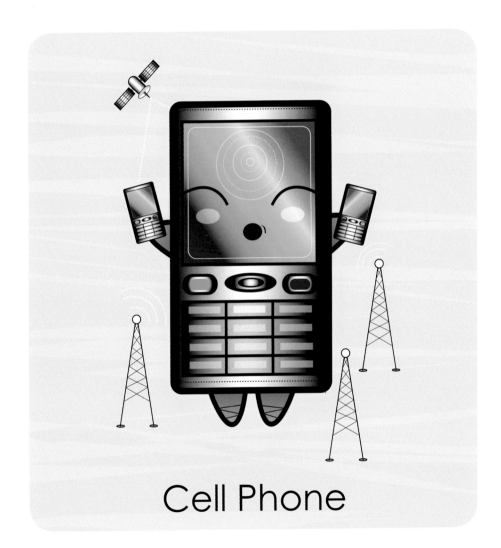

Cell Phone

Computer
Groovy Gizmos

☀ This electronic whiz kid stores and processes all kinds of data
☀ Uses a programmable silicon chip called a microprocessor
☀ Reduces all instructions to simple sums and logic operations

I am the superbrain of this Gizmo groove. Quick thinking and logical to the core, I control the systems that help people operate cash registers, design books, add special effects to movies, and fly planes without the pilot!

I have a user interface, some memory, and—brain of the superbrain—a central processing unit (CPU) that can be programmed to do almost anything. It can crank out an impressive 150,000 million instructions a second! A control unit within the CPU handles the order in which tasks are done, sending and retrieving the results from a block of temporary random-access memory (RAM). A hard disk stores your software, an optical drive reads and writes CDs and DVDs, and a video card processes information for displaying on a screen. Now that's brainpower!

● First computer built: 1938 (Z1, Konrad Zuse, Germany)
● First microprocessor chip issued: 1973 (Intel 4004, U.S.)
● Moore's Law: the number of transistors on a microchip doubles every two years

Computer

User Interface
Groovy Gizmos

* Helpful device that allows control of an electronic machine
* A typical input device is a mouse, keyboard, or touchscreen
* Can also use speech or facial expression recognition

A Groovy Gizmo go-between, I let you talk to computers. Don't let my highfalutin name scare you. "Interface" just means to "be in touch," and "User"—well, that's you, pal!

I'm all about input and output. An input device feeds instructions to a computer, and the computer uses an output device to give a response. Take a pocket calculator. You input the workings of a math problem by punching the keys on the number pad. Hidden from you, the onboard processor calculates the answer. It then displays it on the screen in numbers you can understand. Most input devices use simple prods and pokes (think mouse or keyboard). Outputs are most often visual—a screen or readout, the dials of a car dashboard or a light flashing red on the power plant control panel . . . yikes!

* First graphical user interface developed: 1981 (Xerox Star, U.S.)
* Gorilla arm: the pain caused by operating vertically mounted touchscreens
* Electronic-paper (e-paper) display: Amazon Kindle (2007, U.S.)

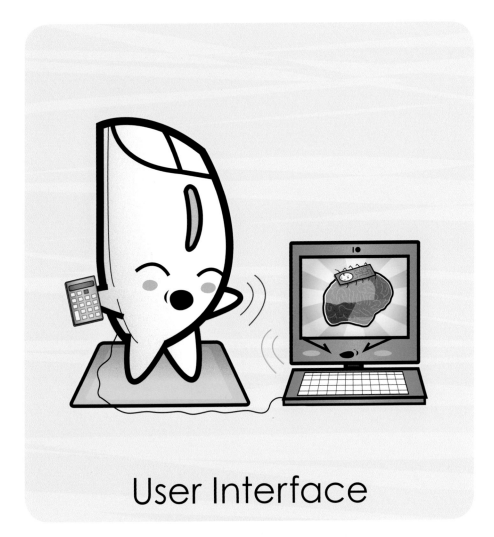

User Interface

Digital Camera
Groovy Gizmos

* Computer-operated camera that creates digital files
* Uses a microchip to convert light into binary code
* Allows live events and news to reach you in record time

My digital eye has seen it all! I'm one versatile dude, finding my way into cell phones, laptops, and telescopes, on the tips of medical probes, and even onboard interplanetary spacecraft.

I store images as digital files, which means I can display them instantly on an LCD screen—no fussy negatives or chemicals here! Pictures are easily edited, cropped, and retouched before being sent by email, posted on the Internet or dispatched via deep-space radio link. My genius lies in a very special microchip called a charge-coupled device (CCD). When photons (particles) of light hit tiny cells on my chip's grid, the light energy is converted into electricity. The chip counts the electrical charge per cell to assess how bright each area of the image should be.

● Invention of CCD: 1969 (Willard Boyle and George Smith, U.S.)
● Pixel count: refers to the number of cells on a CCD chip
● Common picture file formats: JPEG and TIFF

Digital Camera

Flash Memory
Groovy Gizmos

* Lightweight, portable memory used in electronic gizmos
* This upstart has shaken things up in the world of data storage
* Also known as solid-state memory

Whiz, flash, bang! I'm a wizard with compact handiness. Every memory card or stick has my chips nestling inside. I'm used in flash drives, tablet PCs, and slot memory cards—I've even been used in space exploration robots.

I am 100 percent electronic, have no moving parts, and do not require power to save information. This makes my memory "stable" or "nonvolatile." It's a trick that allows me to retain stored data even when the computer is turned off or when your flash memory card is rattling around in your pocket. It also makes me ideal for storing the information that your computer needs to boot up and get running in the first place. Central to my workings is a rewritable flash memory chip, which allows you to add and remove data, quite literally, in a flash!

- Invention of flash memory: 1980 (Dr. Fujio Masuoka, Japan)
- First Memory Stick launched: 1988 (Sony, Japan)
- A USB connector provides power and a data channel for flash drives

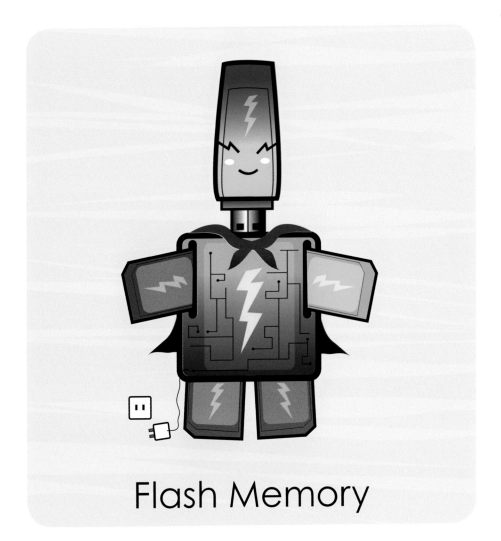

Flash Memory

CHAPTER 5
Super-tech Crew

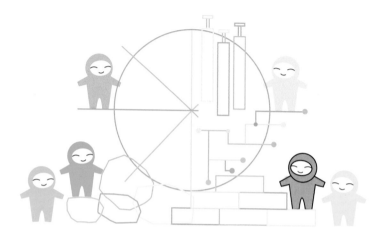

The Super-techs count among the most advanced machines on our planet, each one a leader in its field. Internet, Fiber-optic Cable, and Satellite have changed the way we communicate and access data. They have altered life on Earth far beyond our wildest imagination. Wireless Communication has made life on the move simplicity itself, while Space Suit allows humans to survive the hostile conditions of outer space. Particle Accelerator, the world's largest machine, seeks the smallest parts of matter, while Robot's potential grows by the day. Let's hear what they have to say . . .

Radar

 Satellite

 Laser

 Fiber-optic Cable

 Wireless Communication

 Internet

 Barcode

 Smart Card

 Printing Press

 3-D Printer

 Space Suit

 Robot

 Particle Accelerator

Radar
■ Super-tech Crew

☀ Technology that detects objects by using radio waves
☀ Uses "echolocation," a trick borrowed from whales and bats
☀ Used for defense, astronomy, and weather forecasting

I'm a genuine wartime hero, a real dish! I was invented in the 1930s to warn of approaching enemy aircraft, and I remain dedicated to keeping people safe.

I scan the sky with pulses of Radio's clever airwaves. They bounce off any object they hit, sending a small portion of them back toward my receiving antenna. This allows me to calculate the exact location, direction, and speed of anything out there. Only the most modern stealth technology escapes detection. Today, I have a truly diverse range of applications. I help sea captains detect the shoreline and other ships, and air traffic controllers use me to stack airliners in the sky to avoid collisions. I locate anything from fast-moving missiles to gathering weather formations. In fact, I think I detect a little rain coming!

● First radar: 1934 (Sir Robert Watson-Watt, U.K.)
● Originally an acronym, *RADAR* stands for "radio detection and ranging"
● First radar speed gun: 1954 (Bryce K. Brown, U.S.)

Radar

Satellite
■ Super-tech Crew

❋ Computer-controlled device orbiting planet Earth
❋ Mainly solar powered, but many also have onboard batteries
❋ Used for weather watching, navigation, spying, and research

Peer up into the night sky some time and you might see me. I look just like a star, but gaze for long enough and you'll see that I am on the move, silently circling Earth.

I am blasted into orbit onboard Rocket and then spat out at speeds reaching 17,000 mph (27,000km/h). Once in space, I control my flight path, power consumption, and temperature automatically. I am not alone out here— there's a bunch of us! Weather satellites pass over Earth's poles once every 100 minutes. GPS satellites circle the planet twice a day, while communications satellites as high as 22,236 mi. (35,786km) stay in one position above the surface, rotating in tandem with Earth. But nothing lasts forever: once defunct, we move to a graveyard orbit, adding to the 25,000 pieces of junk that litter space.

● First satellite launched: 1957 (*Sputnik 1*, Russia)
● Most satellites are in low Earth orbit, 100–1,240 mi. (160–2000km) above Earth
● GPS: Global Positioning System, used for mapmaking and navigation

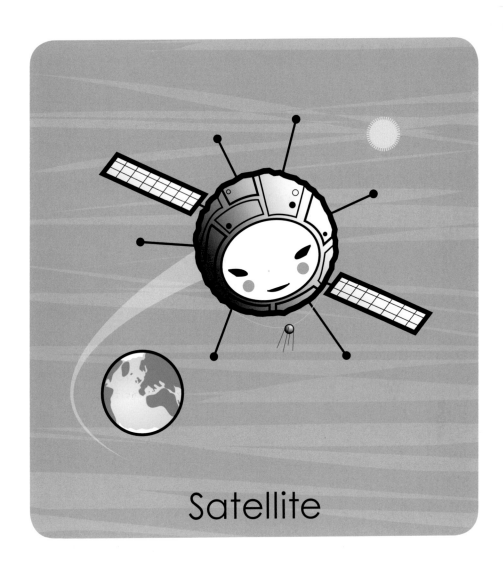

Satellite

Laser
■ Super-tech Crew

✳ Produces monochromatic, coherent, and focused light
✳ Achieves visible, infrared, and ultraviolet frequencies of light
✳ Great for removing embarrassing tattoos and unwanted hair!

Zap! Pow! I'm razor sharp, a vision of the future. Some say I am a little humdrum, what with barcode readers and printers everywhere. But my industrial lasers and scalpels offer the very latest in *cutting-edge* technology.

Unlike the light produced by Light Bulb, mine is strictly a single frequency, which means I produce one color only. My light rays are rigidly organized, too, with all of the photons in step with one another. This is why I make direct beams instead of spreading out. I am created inside a lasing medium, which can be solid crystals, semiconductors, or gases. The medium is pumped with electricity to excite it into producing light, and there I am! Scientists at the U.S. National Ignition Facility (NIF) are trying to use me to create nuclear fusion. Now that *is* the future!

● Number of laser beams at NIF: 192
● Temperatures reached at NIF: almost 90 million °F (50 million °C)
● *LASER* stands for "light amplification by the stimulated emission of radiation"

Laser

Fiber-optic Cable
■ Super-tech Crew

※ Pipe that carries pulses of light by "total internal reflection"
※ Uses include transmission of Internet and telephone data
※ Also used in surgical equipment to bring light inside the body

The big chief of data transmission, I take the lead in global communications. My ultrathin glass fibers carry pulses of light thousands of miles under the ocean.

I am built with a transparent layer of cladding wrapped around a central core. The boundary between the layers acts like a mirror, reflecting light when it hits the sides. This effect bounces light down the tube, guiding waves as they travel along my length. Flashy Laser zaps down my pipes, usually at infrared frequencies. Each pulse is part of a coded stream carrying information—a voice on the telephone or data via the Internet, say. Several streams use the same pipe on different light frequencies, allowing each of my cables an impressively huge bandwidth (capacity). Well, I've always been a big-band fan!

● Typical number of fibers in a cable: 1,000
● Optical cables transmit data at 113,090 mi./sec. (182,000km/s)
● Data rate record: 155 channels, at 100Gb/s, over 4,350 mi. (7,000km) (Bell Labs, Fr.)

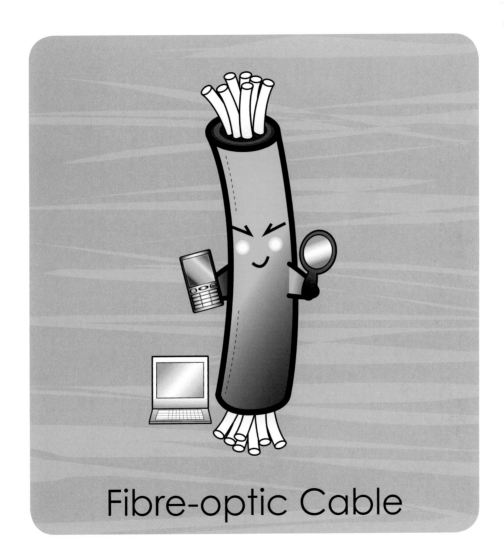

Fibre-optic Cable

Wireless Communication

■ Super-tech Crew

☀ A conjurer that gives radio-linked access to the Internet
☀ Better known as Wi-Fi and Bluetooth
☀ Bluetooth transmits data on 79 fast-changing radio bands

Look, no wires! With my incomprehensible powers, I allow electronic devices to talk to each other *with no physical connection*. Spooky, huh? Not really—your machine just needs a built-in wireless adapter to make it happen.

I use Radio's waves to send messages to a base station as Wi-Fi. This wireless access point provides a gateway to the Internet, through which any wireless-enabled Gizmo can enter. Meanwhile, Bluetooth unites electronic devices, allowing them to share info—swapping files on two phones, for example. Unfortunately, Microwave Oven and cordless Telephone use the same frequency band and can cause interference. *Ring . . . ring . . .* ping!

● Range of Wi-Fi: 65 ft. (20m) (indoors)
● Range of Bluetooth: 16–33 ft. (5–10m)
● Wi-Fi distance record: 260 mi. (420km) (Swedish Space Agency)

Wireless
Communication

Internet
■ Super-tech Crew

❉ A vast network of interconnected computers
❉ Sends requested information as "packets" of data
❉ The World Wide Web is just one of many Internet services

The world's biggest computer network, I am a real know-it-all. I am bulging with useful info and pictures of cute pets. My wires zing with e-mailers, tweeters, and bloggers, buyers and sellers, file sharers, and personal bankers.

Don't confuse me with the World Wide Web. Oh no, I am the whole shebang—the physical parts that make up the global system. I fill warehouses and take the energy of 40 power stations to run. Every device connected to my system has an Internet protocol (IP) address through which it can send and receive packets of data. Each time you access a large server (think Google) you view files on its hard drive. These are sent to your computer in small data packets, and my routers (handling millions per second) have to direct each one to the right computer!

● Invention of the Internet: 1962 (J. C. R. Licklider, U.S.)
● First packet-switching network established: 1969 (ARPANET, U.S.)
● Number of spam messages received each day: 200 billion

Internet

Barcode
Super-tech Crew

* A printed code made from solid bars and gaps
* Commercial products carry a universal product code (UPC)
* UPCs help keep track of stocktaking for stores and businesses

Looking for me? Take a look at the back cover of this wonderful book, dear reader. My classic form is a series of vertical bars whose width and spacing represent a neat, unique, machine-readable number. On commercial goods, this is generally an item code. Read by a laser scanner, I've made supermarket checkouts swift and trouble-free (well, almost).

Barcode

● First scan of a UPC-labeled product: 1974 (Wrigley's chewing gum, U.S.)
● Introduction of the barcoded airline boarding pass: 2005
● Quick Response (QR): 2-D code designed for reading by smartphones

Smart Card

Super-tech Crew ■

✳ Clever critter, AKA a chip card or integrated circuit card
✳ Plastic card with a tiny microprocessor chip embedded in it
✳ This pocket-size safe pair of hands is a mine of information

Smart Card

Be on the lookout for me! A mighty protector, I use tiny Microchip to keep all your data secure. In some countries I'm already used for storing security details on bank cards and medical records on health cards. I can be found in a driver's license or an identity card. How? Well, a card reader connects to my fancy gold-plated contact pads to operate Microchip, and I reveal all!

● Data reading rate: 106 to 848 kilobits per second
● Size of contact area: 0.16 sq. in (1cm²)
● Contactless card: operates using radio frequency identification (RFID)

Printing Press
■ Super-tech Crew

✳ The traditional method used for making printed pages
✳ A highly significant invention for the spread of ideas
✳ The Chinese invented the technique more than 1,000 years ago

I'm an oldie but a goody. Some hail me as the single most influential invention ever! Just think of the newspapers printed every day; all the books in schools, libraries, and stores; this book in your hands. It's certainly im-"press"-ive!

Early versions of me were large wooden screw presses that knocked out 250 pages an hour. They pushed an inked plate onto a blank sheet of paper to make an imprint. Thanks to the development of movable type, pages were assembled more quickly by slotting letters, punctuation marks, and spaces into a grid. Modern-day offset-printing presses are two-story juggernauts churning out 50,000 pages an hour! Color is made by printing on four different color plates.* It's an expensive business, so let's hope there are no mistaykes!**

● Invention of the printing press: around 1440 (Johannes Gutenberg, Germany)
● *Cyan, magenta, yellow, and black (CMYK)
● ** There's one right there!

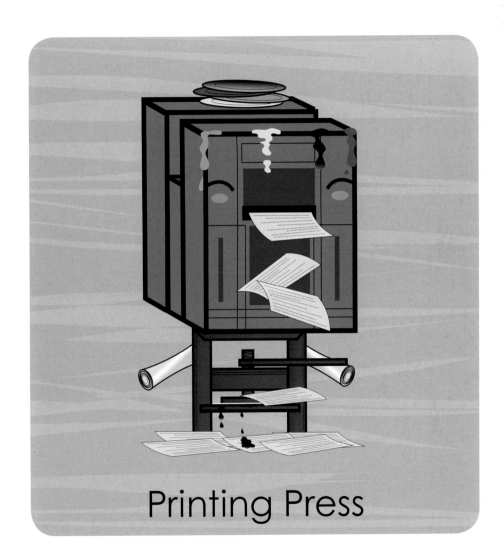

Printing Press

3-D Printer
■ Super-tech Crew

❋ Up-and-coming technology that builds stuff in one piece
❋ This click-and-print marvel is ideal for making custom-made items
❋ Pieces are made of just one material, so recycling is easy

I'm the one to watch. A superstar in the making, I can create 3-D shapes by "printing" them—layer upon thin layer of material—until a solid object emerges.

I'm currently used to make prototypes of manufactured products, but soon I will be producing almost anything you need, right there in your home. Toys, toolboxes and tables, chairs, cufflinks, and coat hangers—if you can draw it, I can print it! (And if you can't draw it, don't worry, Internet will have designs you can download.) I use two processes: direct printing and laser sintering. In the first, I spray a fine film of plastic polymers or thick wax using inkjet nozzles like those in a 2-D printer. For laser sintering, I direct powerful ultraviolet lasers to convert liquid plastic into solid shapes. Oh yes, I'm one "form"-idable dude!

● Size of 3-D dots: 0.002–0.004 in. (0.05–0.1mm)
● Thickness of layers: about 0.004 in. (0.1mm)
● Time it takes to make a plastic 3-D printed flute: 15 hours

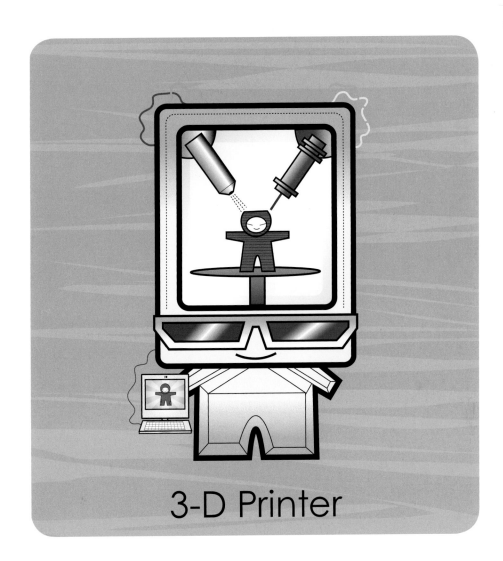

3-D Printer

Space Suit
■ Super-tech Crew

✸ Tough and reliable protection for astronauts
✸ More of a one-person spacecraft than a piece of clothing
✸ Has legs that are color-coded to identify the occupier

I'm a cosmic hero, an outer-space lifesaver. Sure, human bodies are fine-tuned to living conditions on Earth, but get them out here and things get very scary . . . fast!

Going out in space without me is not a good idea! Within minutes, a lack of oxygen knocks you out. You cook in the sunlight (250 °F, or 120 °C) and freeze in the shade (–150 °F, or –100 °C). The lack of air pressure makes your blood boil, and then there's the radiation . . . No, you're better off with me. My modules clip together to make a pressurized suit that provides oxygen and removes carbon dioxide. My hard, fiberglass torso protects your vital organs, and a gold coating on the clear, plastic bubble helmet blocks out most radiation. Between my layers runs a web of pipes carrying water, keeping you cool, calm, and collected.

● Number of parts in a typical space suit: about 18,000
● Number of separate steps to putting on a space suit: 25
● Length of pipes in a typical space suit: 300 ft. (91.5m)

Space suit

Robot
■ Super-tech Crew

* An automated machine dedicated to a life of service
* Has a brain operated by a computer program
* Can be either self-operating or with some operator control

I'm used like some high-tech Cinderella, doing things that humans find too dull, difficult, or dangerous. But I have a brain, you know, and can make decisions for myself.

I mow the lawn, pick fruit, clean out pipelines, sniff out and defuse bombs, help astronauts work in space, find shipwrecks, build cars from scratch, perform keyhole surgery . . . Whew! I even have my own soccer teams. Humanoid robots, such as my heroes ASIMO and TOPIO, mimic humans, but it's very hard to get the mechanics right. It's usually easier not to go on legs, for example, so I often use tracks or rollers. They say that a robot is only a robot if it has a brain (although it can also have an operator). But what about a heart? I'd be a faithful companion—we'd be great friends. Whaddaya say?

● Leonardo's robot: automaton designed by Leonardo da Vinci, Italy, 1495
● Robots in use today: more than 50% Asia; 32% Europe; 16% North America
● Cost of building one ASIMO unit: $1 million

Robot

Particle Accelerator
■ Super-tech Crew

* ☀ A machine that is used to break up atoms
* ☀ Gives subatomic particles energy in the process
* ☀ The smallest parts of matter hold the deepest secrets

A real smasher, I pump pressure onto matter until it spills the secrets of the universe. I'm not talking about atoms here. No, no, no, I'm after the very smallest parts in the mix—the so-called hadrons and quarks.

I get my oomph from super-high energies, which help me break up stable atoms that would rather stay whole. From there, it's simple. I use powerful magnets to accelerate the itty-bitty blips to phenomenal speeds and then slam them into one another inside gigantic detectors! Scientists sift through the wreckage looking for evidence of undiscovered new particles. My Large Hadron Collider zaps particles around a 17 mi. (27km) circular track built 328 ft. (100m) underground. It is colossal equipment for detecting particles smaller than you can imagine!

* ● Grandfather of modern particle accelerators: Rolf Wideroe, Norway
* ● World's largest particle accelerator: Large Hadron Collider (LHC), Switzerland
* ● Particles in the LHC complete the 17 mi. (27km) loop 11,245 times per second

Particle Accelerator

CHAPTER 6
Gearheads and Power Freaks

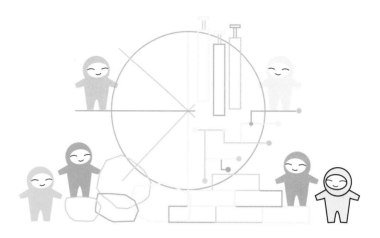

Like you, a machine needs energy to get it moving, and that's a job for this bunch of heavies. The Gearheads are prime movers—engines that convert energy (often from chemical fuel) into motion. The Power Freaks provide, store, and transmit driving force to other machines. But there's a catch! Whether it's the pizza you had for lunch or a handful of plutonium rods, all fuels require you to consider how best to use them. Driving to the store for a gallon of milk slurps up the energy it takes to get a ton of metal rolling down the road. If it's just as easy to walk instead, why not? You might want to work off that pizza!

Sail

Reciprocating Engine

Jet Engine

Rotor

Rocket

Ion Thruster

Electric Motor

Generator

Battery

Fuel Cell

Solar Power

Nuclear Power

Sail
Gearheads and Power Freaks

☀ This prime mover harnesses the energy of moving air
☀ Acts like a wing to lift a vessel up as well as drive it forward
☀ Used for transportation over water, ice, sand, and across space

I'm an old sea dog, a rugged explorer who has traversed the oceans on great voyages of discovery. Unfurling to catch the slightest puff of wind, I take advantage of this free source of energy that swirls around the planet.

Meeting the wind head-on creates a dead zone that leaves me all out of puff. I go slack and flappy and can't propel the craft. But by tacking, or zigzagging, I deflect the wind like an aircraft wing, creating a force that pushes the boat forward. On water, I can go at a fair clip—faster, even, than the wind speed itself—but it's in space that I really go the distance. Using ultrathin mirrors, I catch the steady stream of particles and radiation coming from the Sun. This solar wind can drive spacecraft at cruising speeds of 43 mi./sec. (70km/s)! That'll blow you away!

● Dead zone, AKA being "in irons" : 30°–50° either side of the wind
● Nautical speed: 1 knot = 1.15 mph (1.85km/h)
● First solar sail: 2010 (IKAROS: 2,153 sq. ft. (200 m²), 0.003 in. (0.0075mm) thick)

Sail

Reciprocating Engine
Gearheads and Power Freaks

* Drives motor vehicles powered by gasoline or diesel
* Has a two-stroke, four-stroke, or six-stroke cycle
* Generates electricity without a connection to an electrical grid

I am the workhorse for motorized transportation. Cough, splutter, and wheeze I might, but I've been around the block a few times, and I'm still firing on all cylinders!

A sturdy old-timer, I house a hollow cylinder with a combustion chamber at the top. I burn fuel in here, triggering an explosion that would blow less hardy types apart! The blast sends a piston hurtling down my cylinder —the first of four down and up strokes that make up one of my cycles. The first stroke (down) sucks in air and fuel, while the next (up) compresses the mix. My spark plug fires and BOOM!—a power stroke (down) provides the driving force. The final stroke (up) pushes the exhaust out of my belly. To even out my one-power-stroke-in-every-four motion, I often have several cylinders in the same block.

- AKA internal combustion engine, because it burns its fuel inside the engine
- First successful four-stroke engine: 1876 (Nikolaus August Otto, Germany)
- Average efficiency of a car engine: about 25%

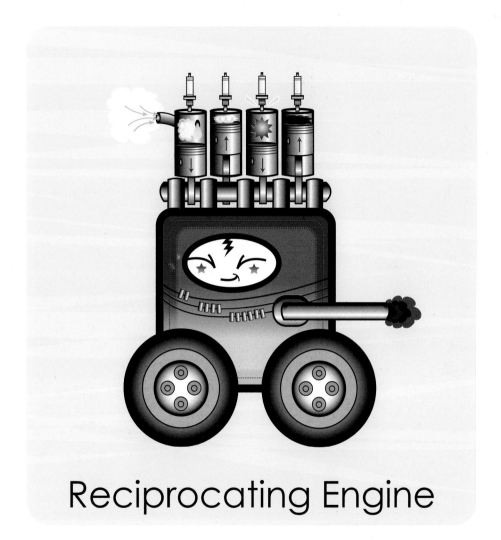

Reciprocating Engine

Jet Engine
Gearheads and Power Freaks

✳ This flyboy powers airliners, fighter planes, and speedy cars
✳ A form of internal combustion engine, AKA a gas turbine engine
✳ Airliners have turbofan engines; fighter jets have turbojets

I'm a speedy highflier who just loves a good blowout! You'll have seen me on an aircraft—slung under the wing or attached to the tail fin—but I also boost motorboats and cars to world speed records. Catch me if you can!

Like wheezing Reciprocating Engine, I burn fuel inside my body, but you won't see me wasting my energy driving pistons! No, I use the force of hot exhaust gases to create thrust. It all starts with whirring fan blades at my front end, which suck air into my combustion chamber and compress it to a tenth of its original volume. Jet fuel is sprayed into the chamber and ignited. The expansion of the exploding mixture sends hot gases screaming out of my rear, and the momentum of this rear-end expulsion creates an equal thrust in the opposite direction.

● First operational jet engine: 1939 (Hans von Ohain, Germany)
● Combustion chamber temperature: 1,000 °F–1,300 °F (550 °C–700 °C)
● Land speed record: 763 mph (1228km/h) (ThrustSSC, U.K., 1997; turbofan)

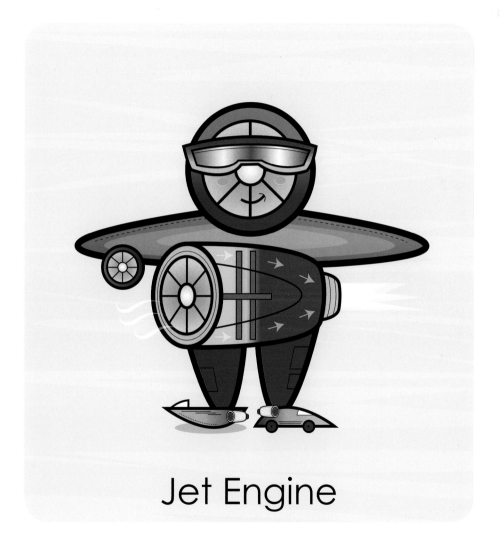

Jet Engine

Rotor
Gearheads and Power Freaks

☀ Horizontally spinning fan that lifts a helicopter into the air
☀ This gyrating Joe is driven by a turboshaft jet engine
☀ When spinning vertically, a rotor pulls a craft forward, not up

I'm a dizzy kind of fellow, a real whirlin' dervish. I'm made up of two to five blades that spin around and around at super-high speed to lift things off the ground.

Each of my blades is designed with a curved leading edge that tapers to the rear. Shaped like long, thin wings, they push the air downward to create a thrust force in the opposite direction (upward). They can be pitched at a steeper angle to give more lift or vertically to pull things forward (think propellers). As well as lift, my rotation creates a force that pushes in the opposite direction to that of my spin. This means that most helicopters need an additional rotor on the tail to keep them flying straight. I can do things that an airplane can't—I can hover, turn on the spot, and fly backward. Neat, eh?

● First successful helicopter: 1942 (Igor Sikorsky, Russia)
● First turbine-powered helicopter: 1951 (Charles Kaman, U.S.)
● Tandem-rotor helicopter: powered by two top-mounted rotors

Rotor

Rocket
Gearheads and Power Freaks

✸ Works by throwing exhaust gases behind it at high speed
✸ Carries all necessary fuel and oxidant onboard
✸ Fuel tanks are jettisoned once spent

5 . . . 4 . . . 3 . . . 2 . . . 1 . . . Lift off! Hold on to your hat, baby, as I blast you through Earth's atmosphere and into outer space. I light up the sky as fireworks, missiles, space rockets, and lifesaving ejection seats in fighter aircraft.

Like my cousin Jet Engine, I'm a reaction engine that operates by throwing mass at high speed out of my rear to produce thrust in the opposite direction. But in the vacuum of space, there is no air to burn the fuel, so I carry oxygen with me. Take a look at your average spacecraft and you'll see a number of thin, pencil-like tubes attached to the sides. These carry solid fuel or liquid propellant. They work like fireworks—once lit, there's no going back . . . Whoosh! Now, that's a reaction I like—c'mon baby, light my fire!

● Speed of exhaust gases at launch: approximately 2.8 mi./sec. (4.5km/s)
● Escape velocity from Earth: 7 mi./sec. (11.2km/s)
● First rocket in space: 1957 (R-7 ICBM, Russia)

Rocket

Ion Thruster
Gearheads and Power Freaks

* Electric propulsion for interplanetary spacecraft
* Reaction engine that uses beams of charged atoms
* Silent and more efficient than a rocket engine

I am the Ion Man! I work using the same stuff that makes balloons stick to your hair and cling to sweaters—charged ions. My abilities are simply astronomical!

An ion is an atom with a positive or negative electric charge. Ions with opposite charges attract each other, and I take advantage of this. I accelerate ions—positive or negative (I'm not picky)—toward a metal plate with an unlike, or opposite, charge. These particles pass through holes in the plate to create beams of super-fast ions that can push a spacecraft forward. While Rocket relies on chucking lots of mass (hot exhaust gases) out behind it, I go for low mass (tiny ions) at blistering speeds. It takes me a long time to get going, but I move along quietly, building speed as the astro-miles flash by.

● First ion thruster mission: 1998 (*Deep Space 1*, NASA)
● Speed of ion exhaust: 31 mi./sec. (50km/s)
● Tank size: 88 lb. (40kg) xenon tank (*GOCE*, 2008)

Ion Thruster

Electric Motor
Gearheads and Power Freaks

☀ A magical device that converts electric energy into motion
☀ Harnesses the power of one of nature's fundamental forces
☀ Small motors power watches; large ones drive ship propellers

I am an electromagnetic wizard! Yes, ladies and gents, before your very eyes I change invisible electricity into motion that pulls, pushes, and spins things around. I may seem commonplace—I open windows in cars, drill holes in walls, and spin discs in DVD players—but think again!

I rely on the incredible phenomenon that a wire carrying an electric current generates its own magnetic field around itself. Make a loop of this wire and you have an electromagnet. Stick the loop next to a second magnet and it attracts to the magnet's opposite pole: a force is generated. If the current traveling through the wire loop reverses direction every half-turn, the magnetic poles flip and the wire loop spins like crazy. Connect the loop to an axle and, voilà, you reap the force—instant power!

● Discovery of principle: 1821 (Michael Faraday, U.K.)
● First practicable electrical motor: 1888 (Nikola Tesla, U.S.)
● The smallest electric motor is made of a single molecule

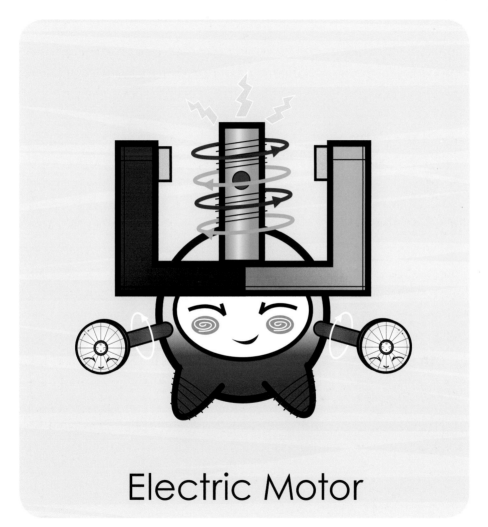

Electric Motor

Generator
Gearheads and Power Freaks

* The booming workhorse of the industrial world
* Converts mechanical energy into electrical energy
* Power plants use steam turbines to drive their generators

A "gen"-uine Power Freak, I operate in reverse to that awful boaster Electric Motor. Extraordinarily powerful, I convert all kinds of mechanical energy into wonderful, tremendously useful electricity. I rule the industrial world!

You can see me in action as the dynamo that powers the lights on your bike, but mostly I toil away in the turbine halls of power plants, heroically providing your house, the streets, and all industries with electrical power. I use an energy source to spin a coil of wire inside a magnetic field, and this sparks up an electric current in the conducting wires. I'm so versatile that I can convert pedal power and tidal power into electricity, as well as that from internal combustion engines, steam turbines, water turbines, and wind-driven turbines. All power to me!

● World's most powerful generator: 700,000 kW (Three Gorges Dam, China)
● World's most efficient gas turbine: 60% (Irsching, Germany)
● World's largest wind turbine: 413-ft. (126-m) rotors (Enercon E-126, Germany)

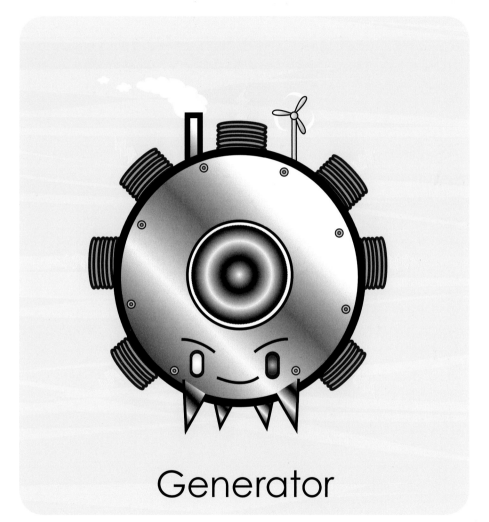

Generator

Battery
Gearheads and Power Freaks

* Converts stored chemical energy into electricity
* Replaced or recharged once chemical reserves are spent
* Potentially toxic, used batteries must be disposed of safely

I'm a portable prince, the pocket whiz kid that runs your wristwatch, calculator, and cell phone. Hook me up to an electrical circuit and a chemical reaction releases electrons from my negative end that then travel around the circuit to my positive end. These moving electrons create an electric current that powers the equipment attached to it. Simple!

Battery

● First battery: 1800 (Alessandro Volta, Italy)
● Cathode: a battery's positive terminal
● Anode: a battery's negative terminal

118

Fuel Cell

Gearheads and Power Freaks

- A special kind of battery powered by hydrogen
- Converts chemical energy in fuel into electricity
- Heralds clean power for cars, buses, boats, and submarines

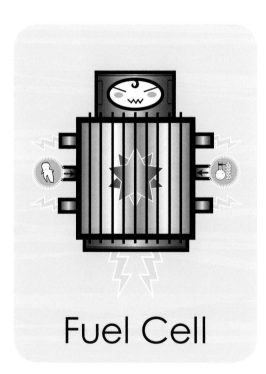

Fuel Cell

I am the green dream. Hug a tree? Man, I love the whole planet! Unlike short-lived Battery, I sup a continuous supply of hydrogen from a tank and take oxygen from the air to power electrical systems. My only other output is water vapor. While that pollutin' Reciprocating Engine chugs away, I run cars cleanly and quietly—a breath of fresh air!

- First fuel cell: 1839 (William Grove, U.K.)
- Efficiency of fuel-cell vehicles: 42%–53% (at full power)
- World's largest fuel-cell power plant: 45 MW (Hwaseong City, South Korea)

Solar Power
Gearheads and Power Freaks

☀ This hotshot converts energy from the Sun into electricity
☀ Earth averages 12 hours of free light and heat each day
☀ Works best in desert areas with few clouds

A little ray of sunshine, I exploit Earth's "stellar" energy source. Every day the Sun bathes our planet in a steady stream of light and heat. Our hot friend provides almost enough energy in one hour to meet the world's needs for a whole year! I help collect it and convert it to electricity.

I have two ways of doing this—with photovoltaic solar cells and in heat engines. Solar cells are semiconducting silicon chips that emit electrons when they are hit by photons of light. Laid out on solar panels, these sunny-side-up marvels can generate electricity for your home. In heat engines, accumulators and mirrors concentrate the Sun's energy to produce steam that can power booming Generator. These solar furnaces can reach temperatures of up to 6,300 °F (3,500 °C)—hot stuff!

● Highest altitude for solar-electric aircraft: 96,863 ft. (29,524m) (*Helios*, 2001, NASA)
● Discovery of photovoltaic effect: 1839 (Alexandre-Edmond Becquerel, France)
● Amount of sunlight absorbed: 19% (atmosphere); 35% (reflected by clouds)

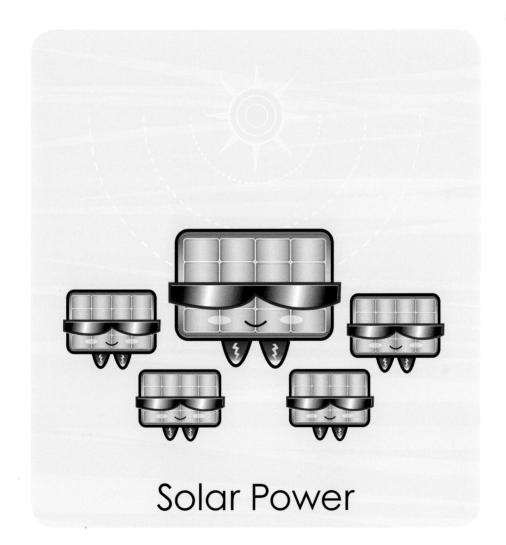

Solar Power

Nuclear Power
Gearheads and Power Freaks

✳ Converts the energy stored in an atomic nucleus
✳ Uranium-235 is nuclear fission's most commonly used fuel
✳ Powers nuclear submarines, warships, and some spacecraft

I may start small but don't be fooled. Compared with other fuels, I am supercharged. I give millions of times more energy than the same volume of oil. I'm an atomic hero!

I access the energy residing at the very heart of matter itself. The nuclei of some heavy, unstable elements split when bombarded by subatomic neutron particles (that's some very small particles indeed). And in splitting, they release a huge amount of energy. This process is called nuclear fission, and the energy is used to generate electricity in power plants and propel nuclear craft. Sadly, with such awesome power comes great responsibility. The fission process also produces radioactive waste that remains lethally dangerous for tens of thousands of years. I'm hazardous, so please be careful.

● First nuclear reactor built: 1942 (Chicago Pile-1, Manhattan Project, U.S.)
● Proportion of world's electrical energy that is nuclear: 13%–14 %
● Half-life of iodine-129 (long-lasting nuclear waste): 15.7 million years

Nuclear Power

INDEX

Lever 6, **16**
Light Bulb 24, **30**, 80

MN
magnetrons 34
Microchip 60, **62**, 66, 70, 72, 89
Microwave Oven 24, **34**, 84
Nuclear Power **122**

OP
oscillators 40
Paper **46**, 90
Particle Accelerator 74, **98**
Plastic **52**
Printing Press **90**
Pulley **18**

R
Rack and Pinion **14**, 22
Radar **76**
Radio 24, **26**, 28, 34, 36, 64, 70, 76, 84
receivers 26
Reciprocating Engine **104**, 106, 119
Refrigerator 22, **32**

Robot 74, **96**
Rocket 78, **110**, 112
Rotor **108**

S
Sail **102**
Satellite 26, 36, 74, **78**
Screw 6, 10, **12**
sensors 22
Smart Card 74, **89**
Smart Materials **58**
Solar Power 78, **120**
Space Suit 74, **94**
Spring **20**, 22, 40
Steel 48, **50**

T
Telephone 24, **36**, 82, 84
Television 24, **28**, 58
Toilet 24, **38**, 58
transistors 62
transmitters 26

UW
User Interface 64, 66, **68**
Wheel **8**, 10, 14, 15, 18
Wireless Communication 26, 74, **84**

GLOSSARY

Accumulator A device such as a rechargeable battery that stores energy.

Additive A way of manufacturing products by building up layers, adding one on top of the other—the opposite of manufacturing objects by removing material.

Alloy A metal blended with other metals or nonmetals to make a material with desirable properties. Alloys include bronze, solder, and steel.

Analog When an electric signal has the same shape as the voice or picture being transmitted.

Atom A tiny particle of matter, made of protons, neutrons, and electrons; the smallest component that can take part in a chemical reaction.

Cellulose A material made from the cell walls of green plants and useful in making paper and fabrics; often obtained from wood pulp or cotton.

Digital When an electric signal is a sequence of binary numbers. Each number is equal to the size of the voice or picture being transmitted at that moment.

Dynamo Another word for a generator—a machine that turns motion into electrical energy.

Electric charge A property of matter that makes charged particles feel a force when they come close to one another. The two types of electric charge—positive and negative—make electricity possible.

Electromagnetism A fundamental force of nature between electrically charged particles.

Electron A tiny, subatomic, negatively charged particle that orbits around the nucleus of an atom.

Element A chemically pure substance consisting of atoms of only one type.

Frequency The rate at which something repeats itself; the number of cycles it makes per unit of time.

Friction A force that slows things down or resists forward movement, often by surfaces rubbing together; also called drag.

Hadron Tiny particles of matter made of quarks bound together. Protons and neutrons are types of hadrons.

Infrared Frequencies of electromagnetic radiation just below that of visible light.

Magnetic field Produced by moving charged particles, changing electric fields, or the spinning electrons of a magnetic material. A magnetic field generates a force felt by charged objects and other magnets.

Mechanical advantage The measure of how much a tool or machine boosts force.

Nuclear Anything relating to the nucleus (core) of an atom. Nuclear fusion is the joining together of atomic nuclei, and nuclear fission is the process of breaking a nucleus apart.

GLOSSARY

Nucleus The central part of an atom, made up of subatomic particles called protons and neutrons.

Oxidant Essential to combustion (burning) reactions, an oxidant combines with fuel to produce heat and light energy.

Particle Often called "subatomic particle," one of the minute parts of matter that group together to make up an atom. All atoms are made of protons, neutrons, and electrons.

Photon A particle of light radiation or electromagnetic radiation. A photon has no mass and no charge.

Photovoltaic The production of electricity by light.

Quark The smallest kind of subatomic particle.

Radioactive Describes an unstable substance whose atomic nuclei break down and release nuclear radiation.

Semiconductor A material that conducts electricity better than an insulator, but not as well as a metal (conductor). These materials are used to control electric current and are the "brains" inside all electronic devices.

Silicon A semiconducting element and the base material for microchips.

Subatomic particle Any part of matter that is smaller than an atom.

Transmission A device in a car that transmits power from an engine to the wheels.

Ultraviolet Frequencies of electromagnetic radiation above that of visible light.